# Our Puppy's Baby Book

Library of Congress Control Number: 2005928242

ISBN-13: 978-0-7645-9578-3

ISBN-10: 0-7645-9578-4

Printed in the United States of America

10   9   8   7   6   5   4   3   2

Book design by LeAndra Hosier
Cover design by Wendy Mount
Illustrations by Robert Pilgrim
Book production by Wiley Publishing, Inc. Composition Services

This book belongs to

_____

who belongs to

_____

# I'm the Pick of the Litter!

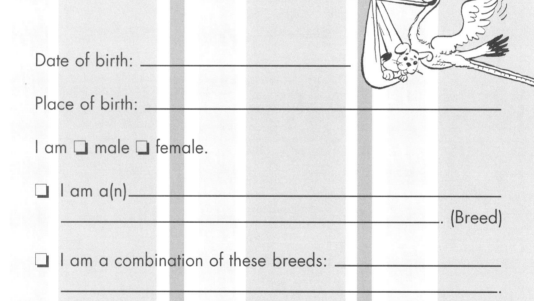

Date of birth: _____

Place of birth: _____

I am ❏ male ❏ female.

❏ I am a(n)_____

_____. (Breed)

❏ I am a combination of these breeds: _____

_____.

# I'm Adopted!

❏ I was adopted from the Humane Society.

❏ I was adopted from this shelter or adoption organization: _____
_____.

❏ I was found and brought home from _____.

❏ I was given to my family by _____.

My history before I was adopted: _____
_____.

# Why I'm So Special

My family picked me because _____.

Compared to my other siblings, I can be described as _____
_____.

❏  I am an AKC registered dog.

❏  My family has a history of show champions.

❏  I have a copy of my family tree:

Mother's name _____

Father's name _____

_____ brothers and _____ sisters in my litter

❏  I come from a diverse and varied background of intelligent and good-looking
dogs. (Don't let my lack of papers fool you!)

# Hey, Good Looking!

My eyes are _____.

My ears are _____.

My coloring is _____.

I have these special markings: _____
_____.

*To make a copy of your puppy's paw print, use scrapbook ink to ink the paw and then press onto the page. Clean off the paw with baby wipes.*

# Homecoming!

Date I came home: _____

My first address was _____.

I share the house with these other pets: _____.

I slept here on my first night: _____.

I ❏ cried ❏ did not cry my first night. I continued to cry for _____ nights.

Now my usual sleeping spot is _____.

I have a
- ❏ doghouse
- ❏ kennel run
- ❏ fenced yard
- ❏ invisible fence
- ❏ big yard
- ❏ small yard
- ❏ crate

*Attach a picture of your puppy in his bed, yard, or anywhere else in his new home.*

# The Truth Behind My Name

My full name is _____.

My nickname is _____.

My family picked this name because _____.

I was named after _____.

Other names they thought about included _____ and _____.

# Winning Personality

The three words my owner(s) would use to describe me are:

1. _____.

2. _____.

3. _____.

Other people who know me (and may not be so biased) would describe me as:

1. _____.

2. _____.

3. _____.

# Fun Time

- ❏ I like to take walks.
- ❏ My favorite place to walk is _____
- ❏ Sometimes I take walks with my friend _____
- ❏ My favorite toy(s) is/are _____
- ❏ I like to play catch with a ❏ ball ❏ Frisbee ❏ other _____
- ❏ I like playing with other dogs.
- ❏ I like to go to the "Bark Park" at _____

*Attach a picture of your puppy playing with his favorite toy, on his leash ready for a walk, or romping with his friends.*

# Chow Time

I eat _____ dog food.

As a puppy, I'm supposed to eat _____ (amount) _____ times a day.

When I'm _____ (age), I can eat _____ (amount) of
_____ (kind of food) _____ times a day.

My favorite treats are _____.

❏ I am allowed these human treats: _____.

❏ I am not allowed any human food.

❏ I am not allowed human food, but _____ sneaks it to me anyway.

I once ate _____.

I stole _____ (kind of food) from _____
when no one was paying attention.

# Check-Up

My vet's name is _____.

The phone number for the vet's office is _____.

The animal hospital for emergencies is _____.

My first visit to the vet was _____ (date).

I ❏ did ❏ did not like visiting the vet.

I acted _____ at the vet.

My favorite part of the vet's visit was _____.

I ❏ have ❏ have not been neutered or spayed.

For my ID:

    ❏ I wear a collar with my ID information.

    ❏ I have a microchip embedded with my ID information.

    ❏ Both.

I have had the following "unscheduled" vet or hospital visits:

_____

_____

_____.

# Getting Big

| Age | Weight | Height |
| --- | --- | --- |
| When I first came home (or at birth) | | |
| 3 months | | |
| 6 months | | |
| 9 months | | |
| 1 year | | |
| 2 years | | |

# Learning the Ropes

For training, I:

❑ go to _____ obedience school.

❑ have a trainer named _____.

❑ am trained by my family.

## Tricks and Commands I Know

| Trick | When I Learned It |
|---|---|
| Sit | |
| Lie down | |
| Come | |
| Stay | |
| Speak | |
| Shake hands | |
| Roll over | |
| Heel | |
| Fetch | |
| Other | |

*Attach a picture of your puppy doing his favorite trick. Or, if your puppy
received a certificate for training, paste it on this page.*

# My Communication Style

When I'm sad, I _____.

When I'm hungry, I _____.

When I want to go outside, I _____
_____.

I know I'm going for a walk when _____
_____.

When I know I'm going for a walk, I _____
_____.

When I want to be petted, I _____
_____.

My favorite place to be petted is _____
_____.

I ❏ have ❏ don't have different cries for when I need to
go out, want attention, or want food.

I am afraid of _____.

When people come to visit, I _____
_____.

If my owner cries or pretends to cry, I _____
_____.

If my owner is mad at me, I _____
_____.

*Attach a picture that illustrates your puppy's unique personality.*

# Outstanding Achievements

❑ I am a show dog. My first show was _____.

❑ I have won these awards: _____
_____.

❑ I have had my picture in the paper on _____ doing _____.

❑ I have done some advertising.

❑ I have been bred and have had these litters:

| Date | Co-Parent | Number of Puppies |
|------|-----------|-------------------|
| _____ | _____ | _____ |

| Date | Co-Parent | Number of Puppies |
|------|-----------|-------------------|
| _____ | _____ | _____ |

❑ I have done these other special things:
_____
_____
_____.

*Attach a picture of your puppy at a show. Or paste in a picture if your puppy has been in the newspaper. You can also paste in show awards or litter information here.*

# Happy Holidays!

My birthday is _____.

I celebrated my first birthday by _____.

I also celebrate these other holidays: _____
_____

Presents I have received include: _____
_____.

I've gotten into trouble during the holidays because I:

❏ tried to open presents.

❏ snatched food from the Thanksgiving table.

❏ chewed up ornaments or other decorations.

❏ peed on the Christmas tree.

❏ Other: _____.

I am included in holiday celebrations in these ways:

❏ I have my own stocking.

❏ I have an ornament with my picture and name on the tree.

❏ I get my picture taken for the family holiday card.

❏ I dress up in a Halloween costume.

❏ I get my own Easter basket.

*Attach a picture of your puppy in holiday finery or caught in the act of opening a present.*

# Looking Good!

I took my first bath on _____.

When I took my first bath, I _____.

I ❑ like ❑ dislike bath time.

My grooming regimen includes:

❑ nail trims _____ times a _____

❑ brushing

Problems I've had with my grooming include:

❑ fleas

❑ allergies/scratching or biting

❑ love to play in mud

❑ slobbering

❑ shedding

❑ Other _____

To avoid bath time, I will _____

_____

*Attach a picture of your puppy getting his first bath. Or include a picture of your puppy after a particularly messy romp through the mud (or after eating a whole Key lime pie off the counter!).*

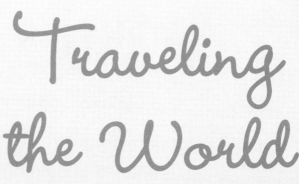

# Traveling the World

I ❏ like ❏ dislike riding in the car.

My favorite place to go for a ride is to _____
because _____.

My first big trip was to _____.

When I can't go on a family trip, I:

   ❏ stay at _____ kennel.

   ❏ have my pet sitter _____ come stay
     with me.

When my family is away, my sitters say that I _____

_____.

*Attach a picture of your puppy on a trip or riding in the car.*

# Troubles and Quirks

I get in trouble for:

- ❏ having "accidents."
- ❏ barking at the mailman.
- ❏ chasing squirrels.
- ❏ sneaking out of the yard.
- ❏ digging up flowers.
- ❏ chewing up shoes or toys that aren't mine.
- ❏ jumping on people or furniture.
- ❏ biting.
- ❏ getting in the garbage.
- ❏ sniffing or "enthusiastically" greeting someone (usually their leg).
- ❏ Other _____

_____.

# Memories

The funniest thing I did was _____
_____
_____.

The thing I got in the most trouble for was _____
_____
_____.

The cutest thing I did was _____
_____
_____.

The biggest mess I made was when I _____
_____
_____.

The thing I did that scared my family the most was

_____
_____
_____.

The thing most people comment on when they see
me is _____
_____
_____.

# My Favorite (and Not-So-Favorite) People

My favorite person is _____.

The person who spoils me the most is _____.

Ways I am spoiled include:

_____

_____

_____.

When someone comes to the door or walks by the house, I _____

_____.

I am ❏ good with ❏ a little wary of kids.

When strangers come up to me, I act _____

_____.

*Insert a picture of your puppy with his favorite person.*

*Attach your favorite picture of your puppy.*

*You may want to paste an envelope onto the inside back cover and use it to
store important papers such as an AKC certificate, family tree, latest vaccinations, and so on.*